The Meanest

THE BENGAL TIGER

THE SCORPION

THE MOSQUITO

THE SALTWATER CROCODILE

THE VAMPIRE BAT

THE KOMODO DRAGON

THE PIRANHA

THE BLACK WIDOW SPIDER

THE MANDRILL

THE ANACONDA

THE PRAYING MANTIS

THE GREAT WHITE SHARK

RANDOM HOUSE 🏠 NEW YORK

Address: India, Bangladesh, Myanmar, Nepal

Size: Almost 10 feet long from nose to tip of tail

Weight: Male: From 375 to 550 pounds
Female: From 220 to 330 pounds

Favorite food: Deer, buffalo, pigs, antelope, gaur, and baby elephants

This killer kitty is armed with dagger-sharp canines—over 3 inches long—that it sinks into the neck of its prey.

The Bengal Tiger

When night falls, the hungry tiger leaves its den to hunt under the starry sky. Its striped coat lets it move about unnoticed among the high jungle grasses.

The tiger steps softly, with its sharp claws retracted so as not to wear them down. They need to stay pointed and sharp as knives. Besides its teeth, these are the tiger's main weapons.

In a single night, a tiger may travel 6–12 miles hunting for large prey. Then suddenly, the tiger makes a 20-foot leap. Buffalo, deer, baby elephants—the jungle is one huge supermarket! The meat-eater begins with the choicest part: the thighs. Its rough tongue scrapes the bones like a file. The tiger often interrupts its feast to drink. It laps up water with its tongue and for a moment looks like a big house cat.

A tiger can eat 80 pounds of meat at one time but needs only around 13 pounds per day to stay fit. With a full stomach, it can spend a whole day sleeping.

When they are about 6 months old, baby tigers start to travel with their mothers and begin to learn the art of hunting. By 1 year, the little cubs are teething on baby boar or fawns—small animals that are easy to catch!

The Scorpion

Weighing not much more than a sugar cube, some scorpions can go a full year without eating!

Its cryptic (or camouflage) coloration and generally small size allow the scorpion to easily hide on the ground. But woe to the person who steps on one!

The scorpion's stinger is located at the end of the tail. As sharp as a needle, it pierces the skin of the scorpion's prey and injects the victim with venom. The sting from some scorpions can even kill a person (although the scorpion's prey of choice are insects and other invertebrates).

Even *being* a scorpion is dangerous. After mating, the males must make a quick getaway: more than half of them are devoured by the females! Held in their vise-like jaws, the males are quickly eaten.

The scorpion uses its hard exoskeleton as a shield and has over 100 pairs of muscles to move its "armor." The shells of some species of scorpion are even said to protect them from nuclear radiation!

Happily, not all scorpions are dangerous. Many species are completely harmless. Out of the 1,500 known species, only 25 have venom capable of killing a person.

North America

Central America

South America

Middle East

Africa

Asia

Address: North America, Central America, South America, Africa, Middle East, Asia

Size: From .5 to 8 inches long (not including its claws)

Weight: Up to 2 ounces

Favorite food: Insects and other invertebrates

North America

Europe

Asia

Africa

South America

Australia & Pacific islands

Address: Wherever there are warm weather, water, and warm-blooded animals
Size: From .16 to .4 inches long
Favorite food: Male: Flower nectar
Female: Fresh blood

In the mosquito family, it's only the female that bites. She needs the blood to provide nutrients that give her the energy to reproduce.

The mosquito's feather-like antennae help her identify the odor and movements of potential victims up to 32 feet away. When ready to strike, the female reveals her stylet and inserts this .1-inch-long syringe into the skin of a bird or mammal. Then it sucks up the animal's blood. Weighted down with a full belly, the female mosquito slowly flies away like a balloon. That's when she's most easily swatted. But of course, it is now too late and the bite is starting to itch! This is because the saliva of the female mosquito contains an anticoagulant—a substance that keeps the blood of her victim from clotting. Very quickly, the anticoagulant causes itching and a big red welt appears on the skin.

In tropical regions rich in swampland, mosquito bites may be dangerous. Mosquitoes can transmit malaria and yellow fever. To avoid catching such a disease, people traveling to these places take oral medications, get vaccinations, and sleep under protective mosquito nets.

Bzzzz! The female flaps her wings 800 times per second while searching for some skin to bite.

The Mosquito

When it swims out to sea, this most ferocious of all crocodiles will even attack a shark!

An excellent swimmer, the saltwater crocodile—the largest of all crocs—often swims out to sea over 350 miles from the coast. It swims silently underwater by moving its powerful tail back and forth.

The saltwater crocodile has an extra pair of transparent eyelids. These protect its eyes when diving, yet allow it to see clearly. It can surprise its victims from directly beneath the waves. Sometimes the saltwater crocodile will jump out of the water to grab a seabird in flight. With its 3.5-foot-long jaws, the predator swallows its prey without chewing.

Underwater, its nostrils and ears are closed over. The reptile can be still and remain underwater for up to an hour. When the saltwater crocodile comes back to the coast, it remains invisible, hidden in the shallow, muddy water. That's when the voracious reptile whips its tail and clamps onto its prey with jaws of steel. It is sometimes a man-eater. Swimmers and sailors—watch out!

India
Papua New Guinea
Malaysia
Indonesia
Australia

Address: India, Malaysia, Indonesia, Australia, Papua New Guinea
Size: From 22 to 30 feet long
Weight: From 1,300 to 2,200 pounds
Favorite food: Any animal that ventures near or in the water

The Saltwater Crocodile

Address: Trinidad, Mexico, Chile, Argentina, Uruguay

Size: From 2.5 to 4 inches long

Weight: From .5 to 1.75 ounces

Favorite food: Cattle blood

THE VAMPIRE BAT

Mother Nature's Dracula, this bat can't go for more than 48 hours without a drink of blood. . . .

By moonlight, vampire bats leave their caves and tree trunks. Without making a sound, they fly low above the ground, looking for sleeping animals (cattle and horses, usually) whose blood they can drink. First the bats sink their teeth into the necks of their prey. Then they use their tongues to apply saliva containing an anesthetic anticoagulant to their victims' wounds. Thanks to this handy technique, the prey do not feel the bites and their blood keeps flowing. The vampire bats then lick the blood that flows from the wounds for about 20 minutes.

When a vampire bat has an unsuccessful hunt, it can count on its friends to share their wealth. Those who have drunk a good meal will spit up some of the blood they have consumed to feed the hungry few.

Vampire bats rarely attack humans. Nevertheless, their bites are dangerous. They can transmit rabies, an infectious disease that always results in death unless treated quickly.

This gigantic lizard can swallow over 6 pounds of meat a minute....

The Komodo Dragon

Indonesia

Address: Indonesia
Size: Up to 9.5 feet long
Weight: Can reach weights greater than
300 pounds
Favorite food: Wild boar and deer

The Komodo dragon is a leftover from prehistoric times. Its ancestors walked the earth 145 million years ago, at the time of the diplodocus!

Even in a heat wave, at 105°F in the shade, the Komodo dragon is on the lookout, ready to attack. Its sense of smell is hundreds of times greater than our own, telling the beast when dinner is nearby.

The Komodo dragon is the largest of all lizards. It is an opportunist scavenger but is also quite capable of hunting live prey. Using its strong jaws, sharp teeth, and claws (which form 2-inch-long spikes!), the Komodo dragon can rip apart a wild boar or deer in a matter of minutes. The reptile has also been known to attack humans.

Since it is an excellent climber and a powerful swimmer, there is almost nothing that can stop it. The worst enemies of the Komodo dragon are brush fires lit by poachers hunting deer and buffalo. Despite its incredible strength and agility, it is unable to run quickly over long distances, so the Komodo dragon dies roasted in the flames.

Of the
60 species
of piranha,
only 3 are
very danger-
ous. The black-
and the red-
bellied piranhas are
two of the worst. They
measure only 2 to 2.5 inches
long but are the most dangerous
despite their small size. The piranha's muscular jaws are armed with sharp, triangular teeth. These
enable it to tear the flesh off its victim with amazing speed.

The scent of blood and the slightest noise will attract
hundreds of piranhas. Their feeding becomes more fierce as
they increase in number. They devour their prey in rapid
bites, each time tearing off pieces of flesh no larger than a
small coin.

Piranhas rid the waters of carrion (dead animals) and sick
or injured fish. This helps prevent the environment from
being fouled.

Central America

South America

Address: Central and South America
Size: From 2 to 19.5 inches long
Favorite food: Carrion and sick or injured fish

When swimming in a school, this freshwater fish is as dangerous as a meat-eating shark!

The Piranha

The Black Widow Spider

No bigger than a chickpea, this wicked web weaver injects a lethal venom into its victims!

Address: North America, South America, Africa, Australia and Pacific islands, Asia

Size: Male: About .3 inches
Female: About .6 inches

Favorite food: Gnats and flies

The female black widow spider can be recognized by her licorice-black body and the blood-red "tattoo" on the underside of her abdomen. A native of warm regions, she loves to nestle in remote corners of houses. She prefers gnats and flies to human victims. After jabbing her 2 syringe-like fangs into the skin of her prey, the black widow injects her poison. The venom immediately attacks the nervous system. It paralyzes and in some cases causes death. (Before the development of antivenin, about 5 percent of humans bitten by the black widow actually died.)

The female black widow is a tough character. She is twice the size of the male and sometimes devours him after mating! Certain males are suspicious and attempt to avoid this fate by giving the females gifts. Like someone giving flowers on a first date, they might offer a female a fly wrapped up in a web! Sometimes this is enough to distract her and save their lives.

The Mandrill

The male mandrill frightens enemies with his African warrior mask!

Africa

Address: Cameroon, Gabon, Congo, Equatorial Guinea
Size: From 31 to 39 inches tall
Weight: Up to 55 pounds
Favorite food: Fruit, seeds, leaves, insects, and small animals

This cousin of the baboon is the most colorful of all mammals. The male's bright red-and-blue mask does not go unnoticed. All of the animals in the forest can recognize and identify it from a distance . . . and when they do, they often run the other way! That's because the mandrill—which can weigh up to 55 pounds—is a dangerous fighter. It usually lives in clans of some 20 to 50 monkeys under the authority of the strongest male in the group.

More discreet, the female mandrills wear a grayish brown mask. *But watch out!* Both the males and females have canines as sharp as those of a wildcat. With a concert of growls and roars, the mandrills box and bite anyone who tries to enter their territory. The leopard is one of the rare predators that dare to attack these monkeys. After a battle, the mandrills renew their strength by gorging on fruit and frogs.

THE ANACONDA

This 450-pound snake can swallow a 7-foot-long caiman whole!

This South American reptile—which can measure up to 30 feet!—can grow to be the heaviest snake in the world. It lurks in murky swampland waters, revealing only its eyes and nostrils. Like all snakes, the anaconda has no ears. Totally deaf, it senses the approach of animals from vibrations on the ground. It often perches in trees to look for prey coming to drink.

The anaconda is not venomous like the cobra. It is a constrictor: it uses its muscular body to wrap itself around its prey. Then, like the boa, it asphyxiates its victims (often tapirs, jaguars, and caimans) by tightening its coils around them.

The anaconda's jaws are capable of stretching and separating from each other. This adaptation enables it to swallow enormous meals in a single gulp. After swallowing a crocodile, the anaconda takes several weeks to digest it.

When they are born, baby anacondas measure about 25 inches long and can already gulp down baby birds!

South America

Address: Swamplands of the Amazon, Guyana, the Orinoco basin of South America

Size: From 10 to 30 feet long

Weight: From 440 to 506 pounds

Favorite food: Fish, tapirs, caimans, and any animal that comes to the water to drink.

Address: North America, southern Europe, Africa, Asia

Size: Male: From 1 to 4 inches long

Female: From 2 to 6 inches long

Favorite food: Butterflies, flies, and other insects

THE PRAYING MANTIS

Sometimes the female mantis hugs her mate so tight, she pops his head off . . . then eats his body!

This ferocious female measures up to 6 inches long, 2 or 3 times as big as the male. When a suitor calls, Ms. Mantis takes advantage of her strength: her forelegs squeeze the male's neck tightly, as if holding it in a vise. Once his head is cut off, the poor male is devoured.

With her mandibles, or jaws, the praying mantis tears her prey apart in a matter of minutes. When not devouring male partners, the females eat the same food as the males: other insects.

Thanks to her beautiful gown—which can change color from green to brown—the praying mantis camouflages herself in high grasses. Unsuspecting butterflies, grasshoppers, crickets, and flies are caught in midair.

Some species of mantis from tropical regions can measure 6 inches long, or the length of a hand. As for the orchid mantis of Malaysia, insects confuse it with a flower and die in the trap of its false petals!

This predator likes meat so much, it sometimes eats other sharks!

The Great White Shark

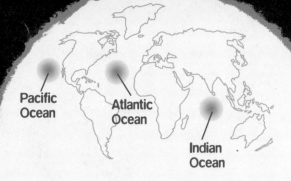

Pacific Ocean

Atlantic Ocean

Indian Ocean

Address: Pacific, Atlantic, and Indian oceans
Size: From 12 to 21 feet long
Weight: About 5,000 pounds
Favorite food: Seals, sea turtles, and dolphins

Once bitten, twice shy! The skin of the great white shark
is covered with thousands of denticles—tiny scales that make it
rough like sandpaper. The great white shark's sense of smell is
highly developed. It is capable of detecting a single drop of blood
in a swimming pool!

For this animal, all flesh is edible. While it may prefer to eat
a seal rather than a surfer, it will take a piece out of most anything
in its path.

All that biting takes a toll on the great white's teeth—during
its lifetime, it may lose over 20,000 of them! Happily (for the shark),
its 3-inch-long triangular teeth always have backup. When one
from the first row falls out, it is immediately replaced by one from
the second row.

After feasting on a seal or dolphin, the great white shark can
go for a full week without eating.

Not all sharks are man-eaters. The basking shark, for example,
eats only plankton.

The Meanest Club

THE KOMODO DRAGON

THE BLACK WIDOW SPIDER

THE PIRANHA

THE VAMPIRE BAT

THE SCORPION

THE BENGAL TIGER

THE SALTWATER CROCODILE

THE ANACONDA

THE GREAT WHITE SHARK

THE MANDRILL

THE PRAYING MANTIS

THE MOSQUITO

Know someone who should join this club? Paste his or her picture here!

Know someone who should join this club? Paste his or her picture here!

PHOTOGRAPHS:
Piranha: left, P. Martin/OKAPIA/BIOS; right, G. Ziesler/JACANA.
Scorpion: D. Heuclin/BIOS.
Mosquito: T. Da Cunha/BIOS.
Bengal tiger: cover, M. Wendler/Peter Arnold/BIOS; interior, R. Puillandre/BIOS.
Saltwater crocodile: left, M. Harvey/BIOS; right, C. Ruoso/BIOS.
Anaconda: T. Montford/BIOS.
Black widow spider: left, D. Heuclin/BIOS; right, J. J. Étienne/BIOS.
Vampire bat: left, J. Sauvanet/BIOS; right, D. Heuclin/BIOS.
Praying mantis: left, J. M. Prévot/BIOS; right, G. Lopez/BIOS.
Komodo dragon: J. Poulard/JACANA.
Mandrill: left, Werner H. Muller/Peter Arnold/BIOS; right, M. Ancrenaz/BIOS.
Great white shark; J. Watt/Panda Photo/BIOS.

First American edition, 2002
Copyright © 2000, 2002 by Les Éditions Play Bac.
All rights reserved under International and Pan-American Copyright Conventions.
Published in the United States of America by Random House, Inc., New York,
and simultaneously in Canada by Random House of Canada Limited, Toronto.
Originally published in France as Les Méchants by Les Éditions du Petit Musc, Groupe Play Bac, in
www.randomhouse.com/kids

Library of Congress Cataloging-in-Publication Data
Doinet, Mymi. The meanest / [Mymi Doinet].
        cm. — (Faces of nature)
                    27 8
                                —Juvenile literature.
                            s. 2. Morphology (Animals). 3. Adaptation (Biology). 4. Animals.]
                            2002   591.6'5—dc21   2001019278

                    February 2002   10 9 8 7 6 5 4 3 2 1
                colophon are registered trademarks of Random House, Inc.